Linux Mint 18

Guide for Beginners

By William Rowley

Copyright©2017 by William Rowley
All Rights Reserved

Copyright © 2017 by William Rowley

All rights reserved. No part of this publication may be reproduced, distributed, or transmitted in any form or by any means, including photocopying, recording, or other electronic or mechanical methods, without the prior written permission of the author, except in the case of brief quotations embodied in critical reviews and certain other noncommercial uses permitted by copyright law.

Table of Contents

Introduction	5
Chapter 1- What is Linux Mint?	6
Chapter 2- Installation of Linux Mint	8
Chapter 3- Linux Mint Desktop	21
Chapter 4- Software Management	42
Chapter 5- Tips and Tricks	63
Conclusion	68

Disclaimer

While all attempts have been made to verify the information provided in this book, the author does assume any responsibility for errors, omissions, or contrary interpretations of the subject matter contained within. The information provided in this book is for educational and entertainment purposes only. The reader is responsible for his or her own actions and the author does not accept any responsibilities for any liabilities or damages, real or perceived, resulting from the use of this information.

The trademarks that are used are without any consent, and the publication of the trademark is without permission or backing by the trademark owner. All trademarks and brands within this book are for clarifying purposes only and are the owned by the owners themselves, not affiliated with this document. **

Introduction

Most people in the world have turned to using Linux as opposed to the common Windows operating system. This is because they have realized how powerful Linux is and that one can achieve a lot when using Linux. One also feels proud when they are termed to be a "Linux Geek." Linux comes in a wide variety of distributions, and each distribution has been made to be used in a particular field for which it is suitable. Linux Mint is one of the available Linux distributions, and this was developed based on Ubuntu and Debian. You can use this Linux distribution to perform a number of tasks. This book is a guide for you on how to use Linux Mint, and it has been updated to Linux Mint 18.0. Enjoy reading!

Chapter 1- What is Linux Mint?

Linux Mint forms one of the common Linux distributions used worldwide by millions of people. This Linux distribution offers full multimedia support and is easy for one to use. It is open source, which means that one can download it and then perform some customizations on it so as to meet their needs. The development of Linux Mint is community driven, which means that the user is able to give back feedback on their experience when using Linux Mint for the purpose of improving it.

The development of Linux Mint is based on Ubuntu and Debian, and it comes with the best packages, up to 30,000 of them, with the best package manager. The first version of Linux Mint was released in the year 2006 as Linux Mint 1.0, and this was a beta release. Later on, Linux Mint 2.0 was released, and this used Ubuntu as its codebase.

In 2010, the Debian-based version of Linux Mint was released. This version of Linux Mint was not tied to the Ubuntu packages.

Chapter 2- Installation of Linux Mint

The Linux Mint operating system can be downloaded for free. This will be downloaded in the form of an ISO file which you are able to burn on a DVD. The liveDVD is bootable and has a fully-functional operating system which you are able to try without having to alter your PC. It is good for you to first try the liveDVD and then install Linux Mint if you like what you see in it. All the tools you may need, including the ones for partitioning, will be available on the DVD. The first step is for you to begin by downloading the ISO of the OS which you can find at http://www.linuxmint.com/download.php. You will then be able to choose the version you need. In this book, we are only interested in Linux Mint 18. This will be found in this download page, so go ahead to download it. The page will also have the following:

- a torrent link

- how to verify the ISO
- a list of the download mirrors

In this case, we need to download the ISO of the file. There are two ways that we can download this, by torrent, which provides a peer to peer protocol, and by a download mirror, which uses either the FTP or the HTTP protocol. The SHA256 checksum will help you know whether your image is corrupted or not once the download is complete.

Once the download of the ISO image is complete, you should go ahead to burn it to a DVD. If the DVD has some faults, you will experience difficulties when trying to boot from it, and finding help will be hard for you. An error in the downloaded ISO file may also make you experience difficulties when trying to boot from it. Errors may also occur as you burn the file to the DVD, and these may give you a headache when trying to boot from it.

The SHA256 checksum will work to help you verify whether the file is as it should be. This verification should be done before you can burn the image to the DVD. The sha256 checksum comes installed with all the versions of Linux. Open your terminal, and use the "cd" command so as to navigate to the directory in which you have kept the downloaded file. Once you are in that directory, type the following command:

sha256sum -b linuxmint.iso

The command will give you a series of numbers and letters, and these represent the checksum for your ISO file. If your ISO file is changed slightly, then the checksum will change drastically. This is why we have to verify and be sure that it is the same.

The link labeled "verify your ISO" on the download page for the ISO has a checksum, and you should compare the one obtained above with this one. If you find that the two checksums are the same, then you should conclude that your ISO file is okay, and then you can proceed to burn it to your DVD.

For those using Windows, it is most likely that you have not installed the sha256sum. You can download and then install it on your system. Both the ISO file and the md5sum.exe should be kept in the same directory. You can then navigate to the directory you have kept these two in via the command line and then type the following command:

sha256sum linuxmint.iso

You will then have a chance to compare the two checksums. Now that you have done the verification, and probably you are sure that the ISO image is okay, you can proceed to burn it to the DVD. Just insert it into the drive and then begin to burn the image to the DVD. For Linux users who want to burn the image to the DVD via the command line, you can run the following command:

cdrecord -v -dao dev=1,0,0 linuxmint.iso

Ensure that you are in the directory in which you have downloaded the file. Ensure that the number dev= has been replaced with the correct number for the device. If you don't know the device number, just run the command given below:

cdrecord –scanbus

You can proceed to burn the image to the DVD.

Boot the LiveDVD

Insert the DVD into the drive, and then restart your computer. The following screen will be seen:

[Linux Mint boot screen: "Automatic boot in 2 seconds..."]

In case you fail to see the screen, the reason is because you have not configured the BIOS settings of your computer so as to boot from the DVD. You can restart the computer and then restart the computer and then the key which commands your computer to boot from the drive. This can be F1, F2, or the Escape key, depending on the computer you are using.

You can then choose "Start Linux Mint" and then hit the Enter key. The live system will be started and you will see its screen. The live system will be ready after some minutes, and the desktop will be presented.

Note that at this point, Linux Mint will not be installed on your computer, but it will only be running from the DVD. However, once you install it on your computer, it will just be the same as the one which you are running from the DVD. Also, you should know that the system will be slower when running it from the DVD than after you have installed it on the computer. The reason behind this is that the data has to be read from the DVD, rather than reading it from the hard disk, which is a bit faster.

Click on the "Install Linux Mint" icon which is located on the desktop. The installer will then appear. It will also be good for you to read more about the release notes so that you can know more about the features, as well as how to tackle any issues which may arise.

Choose the language which you need, and then click on "Continue." A screen which asks you whether you need to install the third party software will be presented. This refers to the software which is not fully open source but it has some conditions for licensing. If you need to use these, just check the box and then click on "Continue."

In our next step, laptop users should ensure that they are connected to a power source, an Internet connection, and that the recommended amount of disk space is available. You can then click on "Continue."

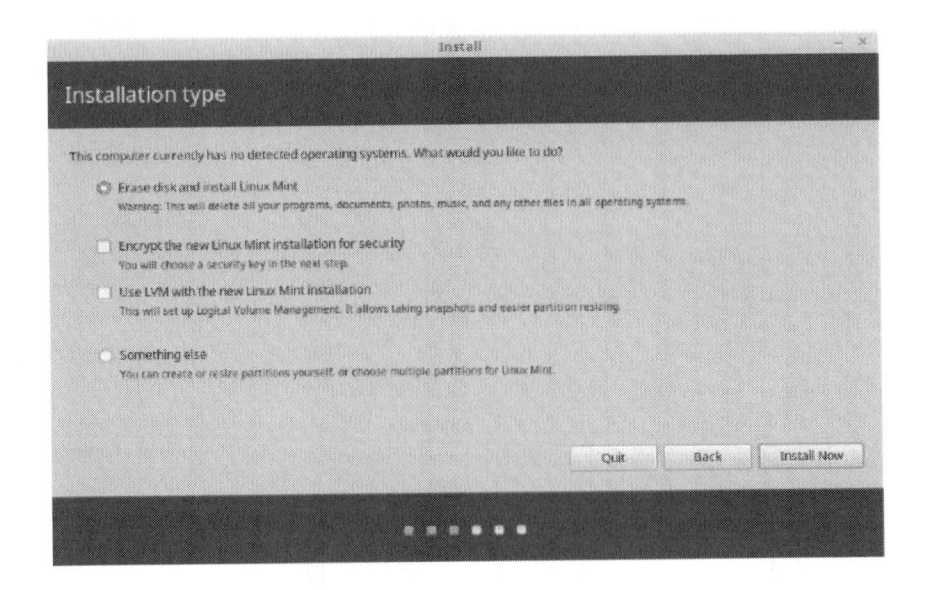

You will then have the option of assigning the whole of your hard disk to Linux Mint, or choose to install it alongside another operating system. You can also choose to assign the partitions in a manual manner. However, it is good for you to be aware that if you choose the entire hard disk, anything in the disk will be deleted and replaced by Linux Mint.

If you choose to install it alongside another operating system, the installer will make use of the available disk space, and the rest will be left for your other operating system. If you choose the option to partition your drive manually, then the partition editor will be presented to you, and you will have to partition the disk manually.

Once you have selected the option which you need, click on the button for "Install Now." The installer will be going in the background, and you will be asked some of the setup questions.

From the map, click on the location for the city which is near to you. This will help in selecting the time zone you are in. Adjust the time to the correct one and then click on "Continue."

It is now time for you to choose the kind of keyboard you will be using. If you are not sure of your keyboard type, begin to type in the text field which is located at the bottom. Keep observing this text field so as to be sure that the key you type is the one which appears on it, and this will tell you whether you have selected the right keyboard or not. Once done, click on "Continue" button.

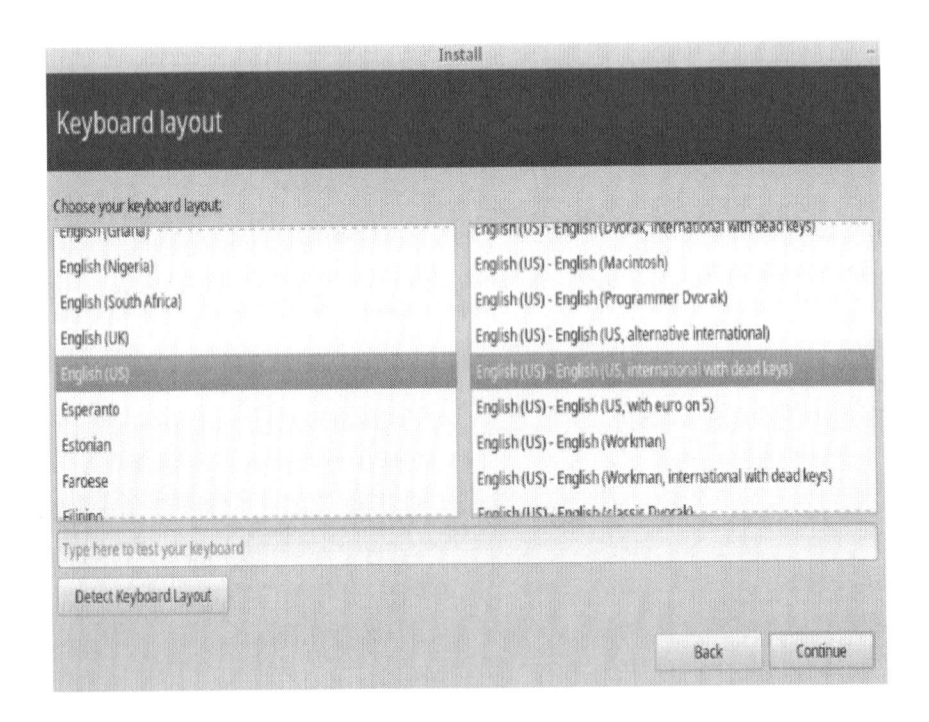

You can then type in your actual name, and the username, as well as the password. Every time that you need to use Linux Mint, you will have to use this username and password so as to login. After the installation of Linux Mint, you will be in a position to define other accounts if there are other users of the system. You can also give the computer a name which will be used for establishing network connections. Once you are through with this, click on the "Forward" button.

If there are other operating systems in your computer, the installer will detect them and then ask you to migrate some of your personal information from it. If you are interested in this, just allow it and then click on the "Continue" button.

The installation will then continue for about 10 to 15 minutes. A progress bar will be shown so as to show you the amount of time which is remaining for the installation to complete.

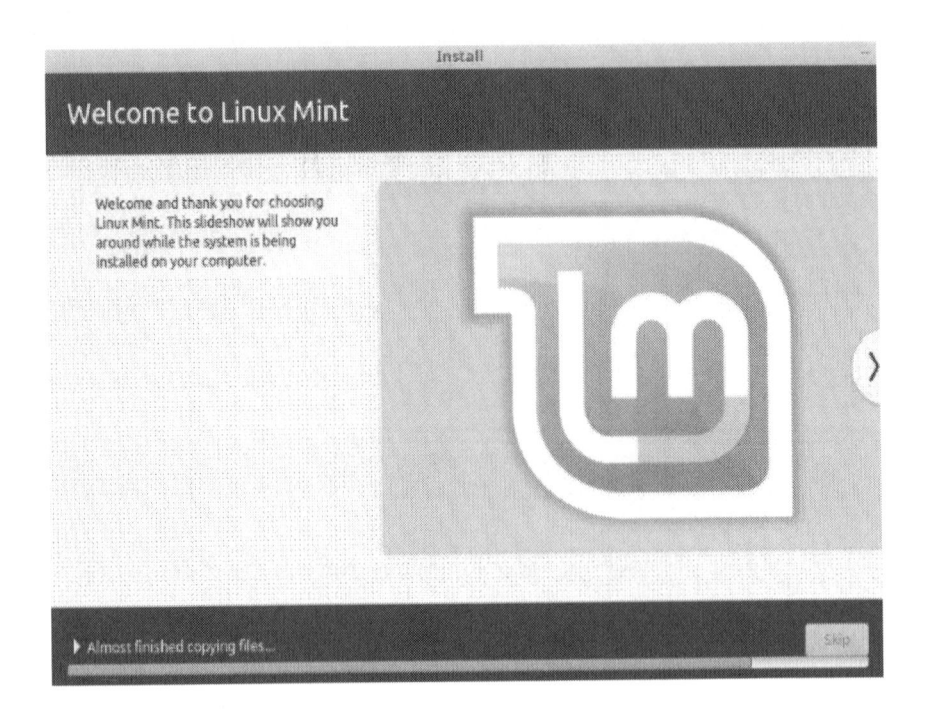

Once the installation of Linux Mint has been completed, click on the button for "Restart Now" and your liveDVD will be shut down. You will be prompted to eject the DVD, so just hit the Enter key and it will be removed. The system will then boot from the Linux Mint which you have just installed.

Chapter 3- Linux Mint Desktop

The Desktop refers to a part of the operating system and it is responsible for the elements which you will see on the desktop. These include the Wallpaper, the Panel, the menus, the Control Center, and others.

Cinnamon Desktop

Cinnamon Linux Mint makes use of the "Cinnamon" desktop, which is very powerful and intuitive.

Desktop Settings

The Desktop is a menu for allowing you to change the aspects of the Cinnamon Desktop which you will mostly be using.

To launch it, click on the "Menu" which is located at the bottom-left corner of the screen, choose "System Settings," and then click on "Desktop."

Linux Mint comes in with a default Cinnamon menu. If you need to launch the menu, click on the "Menu" button which is located on the bottom left corner of the screen or hit the "CTRL+SUPER_L." The SUPER_L on your keyboard refers to the left Windows key.

"Places" Menu

Once you choose the section for "Places," you will be presented with five entries. These entries will provide you with easy access to some of the places on your Cinnamon desktop.

It is the one which will show the storage volumes which you have in your computer. If you had mounted all the partitions in your computer and you have set the "Desktop Settings" to show the "Mounted Volumes" on your desktop, then there will be no need for you to access the Places on a regular basis. However, for those who chose not to show the mounted volumes on the desktop, or who need to do some mounting on a partition which had not been mounted before, you will have to access this place as it is useful to you.

The "Home" place is one of the places which will prove to be useful to you. For those who have been using the Cinnamon desktop in the past, you must be used to clicking on the "Home" icon which is located on the desktop. Once you have opened too many windows and the desktop disappears, the menu will help you to be able to access the "Home" very quickly.

The "Home" folder provides you with a location on your system in which you can store all the data which is personal. The "Desktop" folder represents all the data which you have kept on the desktop. If you place some data on this folder, it will also be added to the desktop. You can also do the same by dragging your file to the desktop. The "Network" place is responsible for showing you the shared devices, domains, and other computers as well as the workgroups which are available on your computer. The "Trash" place is responsible for keeping the files which have been deleted.

After right clicking on a file, you will be provided with two options, namely, "Delete" and "Move to Trash." In case you select "Delete," this file will be deleted permanently, but if you select "Move to Trash," this file will simply be moved to the "Trash" place, and you will be able to access this from the menu. If you need to restore the file, it will be possible for you to drag and drop it to where you need. If you need to permanently delete all the items which are contained in the trash, you will have to choose "Empty Trash," and the files will be deleted permanently.

"System" Menu

The menu provides us with a number of system choices. They are good in providing us with quick access to the most important features of your system. It is not possible for any unauthorized user to access these because a password will be needed for you to gain access.

The button for "Software Manager" will open the Linux Mint Software Manager. It forms the best program for the installation of software in Linux Mint. For you to gain access to the system rights, you will be asked to provide a password.

The button for "Package Manager" will open an application known as "Synaptic." This package is responsible for management of the apps which have been installed on your computer, as well as the ones which are available in the repositories.

The button for "System Settings" opens the Cinnamon Control Center. The app allows us to configure each and every aspect of the Cinnamon desktop as well as the whole computer in general. Let us discuss the items which are contained in this control center.

The "Terminal" button opens an application named "Terminal" which allows one to use the keyboard for entering commands. For those used to the Windows OS, this might be a bit complex, as its command prompt has not progressed much. The Linux Mint terminal is very powerful, and it becomes too easy if one gets used to it. It is worth it for you to know that any command which you run via the graphical desktop in Linux Mint must go through the terminal. A good example is when you click on an icon on the desktop. In this case, Cinnamon is instructed to pass some textual information to the terminal. The terminal can help you achieve a lot with just a single command, as opposed to achieving the same by opening several windows.

The button for "Lock Screen" is used for locking your screen. For you to unlock it, you will be prompted to enter the password. When you click on the "Logout" button, a popup which will allow you to logout or switch the users will be launched.

The "Quit" button will launch a dialog box which allows you to choose what you need. The "Suspend" option will save your session to the RAM, and the computer will sleep until you have pressed a key. The "Hibernate" option will save the session to the hard drive, and the computer will shut down. The "Restart" option will restart the computer. The "Shut Down" option will turn off the computer.

"Applications" Menu

A Linux Mint DVD is usually compressed, and it usually has about 3GB of data. The applications which come installed by default after the installation of Linux Mint are part of the "Default Software Selection."

Note that Linux Mint is developed so that the users can find it easy for them to use it. This is why it comes with some default software installed so that the user can be able to accomplish some of the basic tasks. All the installed applications can be found on the menu's right hand section. The apps have been organized into categories. The first of all the categories is known as "All applications," and it will give the list of all the apps which have been installed.

The other two categories are "Preferences" and "Administration," and they show the applications and the tools which are useful for the configuration and administration of Linux Mint.

In the section for "Accessories," the following is some of the software you will find:

1. Archive Manager- this is the tool for viewing, creating, and extracting the archive files.

2. Calculator- this is simply a calculator.

3. Character Map- this is a tool for easily copying special characters.

4. Disks- this is a tool for showing how the partitioning of the hard disks has been done.

5. Files- this is a link for opening the home directory in the Nemo.

6. Front Viewer- this is a tool for looking for the available fonts.

7. Help- a tool for showing a suitably formatted document which is comparable to this document.

8. Passwords and keys- this is for management of password and the other keys.

9. Screen reader- this helps us to access the graphical desktop environment, a refreshable Braille, or a synthesized speech.

10. Screenshot- this tool helps us take screenshots. To launch it alternatively, you may use the "Print Scrn" key on the keyboard for taking screenshots of the desktop, or "ALT" + "Print Scrn" if you need to take screenshots of the current window.

11. Terminal- this will open the terminal.

12. Text Editor- this is the Gedit, which is a text editor.

13. Tomboy Notes- this is an application to allow you take notes.

14. USB Image Writer- this is a simple tool which helps us write ISO images to the USB drive.

15. USB Stick Formatter- this is a simple tool for cleaning and formatting a USB drive.

The "Education" section provides the following:

1. LibreOffice Math- this is for creating and editing scientific formulas and equations.

The "Graphics" section will provide you with the following software:

1. GIMP Image Editor- this is an application which will allow you to modify, create, or convert pictures. It can be seen to be the same as Photoshop in Windows.

2. Image Viewer- this refers to the Gnome Image Viewer.

3. LibreOffice Draw- this is a graphics application.

4. Pix- this is an application for viewing and organizing images.

5. Simple Scan- this is a tool for capturing images from the scanner.

The "Internet" section will have the following software:

1. Firefox Web Browser- this is a web browser.

2. Hexchat- the IRC chat system. This has been configured so that it can connect you to the Linux chat room by default. It is good for those who need to communicate with Linux Mint users.

3. Pidgin Internet Messenger- this is an Internet messenger. This can be connected to AIM, Gadu-Gadu, Google-Talk, Bonjour, GroupWise, ICQ, IRC, MySpaceIM, QQ, MSN, SIMPLE, XMPP, Yahoo, Sametime, and Zephyr

4. Thunderbird Mail- an application for Email.

5. Transmission- a torrent client.

The following is the software you will find in the "Office" section:

1. Document Viewer- this is a tool for viewing PDFs as well as other documents.

2. LibreOffice- this is a general starter for the office suite.

3. LibreOffice Base- a database application.

4. LibreOffice Calc- this is a spreadsheet application, similar to Excel in Windows, and is compatible with XLS.

5. LibreOffice Draw- this is a graphics application.

6. LibreOffice Impress- an application for making slides for presentation. Similar to PowerPoint in Windows.

7. LibreOffice Math- a tool for creation and editing of mathematical formulas.

8. LibreOffice Writer- a word processor, similar to Microsoft Word in Windows.

The following is the software to find in the section for "Sound & Video":

1. Banshee- this is a music application for playing online radio, and streaming online music services from the Internet. It will also allow you to listen to your music you have kept in a collection.
2. Brasero- this is an application for burning CDs/DVDs. You can also use it for the purpose of making audio CDs from multimedia files.

3. Videos- Totem video player.

4. VLC media player- this is a video player, and is capable of playing almost all types of videos which are available on the web.

The "Search" Field

This is a feature which will provide you with access to an item which you have forgotten where you can find it, or the one you want to access quickly. You just have to click on the Menu which is located on the bottom-left corner of your screen and then begin to type the name of the application which you are looking for. As you continue to type, only the applications which match the words you have typed will be visible on the menu.

This menu will also allow you to define some of your favorite applications and then keep them on a special menu so that they can be accessed easily. From the menu, right click on the application which you like and then choose "Add to favorites." Also, you may have to choose "Remove from favorites." The part with the favorites will be shown on the left of the menu. It is also possible for you to organize how these elements are laid out. You just have to drag and then drop them, and they will be reorganized in the order that you like.

Making Shortcuts

For those who don't like or are not interested in having the "favorites" section, you can achieve a quick access to the elements from the desktop or the panel. Simply right click on the application you want and then select "Add to Panel," or "Add to desktop."

Changing Menu Appearance

There are a number of ways that you can customize the menu. Just right click on the "Menu" and then choose "Configure." You will see the configuration tool for the menu will be presented. You will be given a chance to modify the aspects of your Cinnamon menu.

Restoring Default Settings

If you need to get back to the default settings, from the configure menu, just click on the button which is located on the right of "Remove" and then select "Reset to defaults."

Automatic Launch of Applications

The application named "Startup Applications" can be found under the Preferences. It is possible for you to add an application here. The menu editor can provide you with the right information which you need for the application. If you do this, the application will be launched automatically whenever you start the PC. If you need to disable this, you just have to deselect the app.

Chapter 4- Software Management

Package Management

For those who are using Linux Mint for the first time, you may not be aware of how to organize your software into a "package." This is a very good feature when it comes to security and the ease of access.

Linux Mint has been made in such a way that any hardware attached will be automatically detected and all the drivers are automatically installed. It has also been made possible for the user of Linux Mint to be in a position to do most tasks without having to look for any third party software. The installation of Linux Mint also comes with a fully working office suite, a quality and professional image editing solution, IRC and IM clients, several media players, a disk burner, and many other useful accessories. These are all free software!

There are a number of problems when you are looking for software to use on your Linux system from third party websites. First, it becomes difficult for you to know whether the software has been tested and that it has been proved to be compatible with your operating system. Also, it is difficult to know whether the software will be compatible and then work as you expect with the rest of the software in your system. The software might also be coming from an unknown developer, and you are not sure whether the software will harm your computer or not.

You may be downloading and installing multiple and different programs from different vendors. However, the problem with this is that you will lack a managerial structure in your system. Also, it is good for you to come up with a plan on how you will ensure that the pieces of software you are downloading onto your system will be kept up to date. Sometimes, you may get tired with a certain program. How will you get rid of the program? Some software programs do not offer options for removing them once they have been installed, and even if they may come with it, the program will not be fully removed from the system. What this means is that after you ran the installer for this program on your computer, it took some control of your computer, not forgetting that the program was written by a stranger.

In such a circumstance, the software which has been distributed in such a manner becomes static. This means that you will have to first download the program itself, and then the data libraries which are necessary for it to run. The developer of the program is now aware of the software and libraries which you have installed on your system. This means that for them to make sure that you run the program successfully on your system, they have to supply the program itself as well as the data libraries to you. The download itself will be too big, and whenever you need to update it, you will have to do it or the program itself as well as for the rest of the libraries. This will also be done separately as opposed to doing it at once. This means that with distribution of the static software on your system, there will be the duplication of unnecessary work.

In Linux Mint and other Linux distributions, package management has been used for long and it is the best method for management of software and sorting out of these issues. It provides a safe and automatic installation of software.

The Software Manager

This provides us with the easiest way for installation and management of software. This is built on top of package technology but makes everything easy for us as it allows us to install the individual programs rather than the packages. However, it is good for you to be aware that this uses the package technology in the background, meaning the same benefits will be provided.

To use it, launch the Menu and then click on "Software Manager." The Software Manager will allow you to browse for the software which is made available for Linux Mint. The browsing can be made by category, the search made by keyword, or the software can be rated based on popularity or by rating.

Synaptic & APT

If you need to install more than a single app or you need something which is not provided in the Software Portal or in the Software Manager, there are two other ways which are provided by Linux Mint for installation of the software. These include the "Synaptic," which is a graphical tool and the "APT," which is a command line tool. We will demonstrate how these can be used for installation of Opera:

Begin by opening the Menu and then clicking the "Synaptic Package Manager." Click on the button for "Search," and then type in "Opera." A list of packages will then be presented to you. Navigate through this list so as to identify the one which corresponds to the Opera web browser and then click on it. Tick the box which corresponds to this option, and then choose "Mark for Installation." Lastly, click on the "Apply" button.

To do the same by use of the APT command line tool, follow the steps given below:

Begin by opening the menu, and then click on "Terminal." Type the command given below:

apt install opera

However, you should ensure that you have closed the synaptic before you can begin to use the APT. This is because the synaptic usually uses the APT in the background, meaning that it is impossible for you to run the two simultaneously. The same will apply for the software manager.

As you must have noticed, the use of the APT is much easier, but it does not provide a graphical user interface. If you are a Linux beginner, you may prefer to do things via the graphical user interface, but with time, you will appreciate the power of the terminal and how it makes things easy and fast for you. Sometimes, you may also find it impossible for you to access the packages which belong to a particular application.

The difference with the Software Manager is that it allows you to install the applications by obtaining the packages which are right or you. This will not be done from the repositories (packages databases) which the APT and the Synaptic are able to access but as well as from the other places which can be found from the Internet.

The Software Manager can be used mainly for two reasons:

1. If you are not used to the use of APT or the Synaptic.

2. If the application you need to install cannot be accessed from the APT or the Synaptic.

Removing Applications

The APT is one of the easy ways we can use so as to remove applications. Also, this is the command line, and it makes things easy for us as you are going to see. Remember that we had installed the Opera web browser in our system. Let u try to remove this via the APT. Open the menu and then click on Terminal. Type the following command on the terminal:

apt remove opera

Again, before you can use the APT, ensure that you have closed the Synaptic. This is because the Synaptic is using the APT in the background, and it will be impossible for you to make use of the two.

With execution of the single command given above, Opera will have been uninstalled from your system.

Synaptic

Synaptic can also be used for the purpose of uninstalling packages. Let us demonstrate how one can achieve this.

Begin by opening the menu and then clicking on "Package Manager." Click on the button for "Search" and then type in "Opera." You can then navigate through the list which is provided, and then find the option which is corresponding to the Opera web browser which we installed earlier on. Tick the box which corresponds to this option, choose "Mark for Removal," and then click on the "Apply" button.

Updating System and Applications

After a new version of a package you have installed on your computer has been made, it is possible for you to upgrade it to the new version. The update can be in the form of a security update to a component of your operating system, or the optimization of a specific library or you may need to update to some new version of the Firefox browser.

The Linux Mint system is made up of packages, and the update to this system can be done by updating any part of these packages. Once you do, the old package will be replaced with the new package.

In Linux Mint, a number of ways exist that one can update their packages, but we recommend that you use only one of those ways.

The APT can be used for upgrading the system by use of a single command which is "apt upgrade" but this is not recommended. The problem with this is that no distinction will be made on what you need to upgrade, and everything in your system will be upgraded.

You should note that some of the parts of the system are up to date while the others are not. Consider the situation in which you upgrade your kernel, which is the part which directly communicates with the hardware. If you do this, your sound support might be broken, the support for the wireless card as well as the other applications like the VirtualBox and the VMWare as they are closely connected to the kernel.

The Update Manager

The Update Manager is a tool which comes with Linux Mint. It is responsible for providing the user with information regarding updates, and the user is also allowed to specify how secure an update should be before it can be applied. This means that it works to shield you from security vulnerabilities.

If the mouse pointer is placed on top of this, then you will be informed of whether your system is up to date or not, and the number of updates which are available.

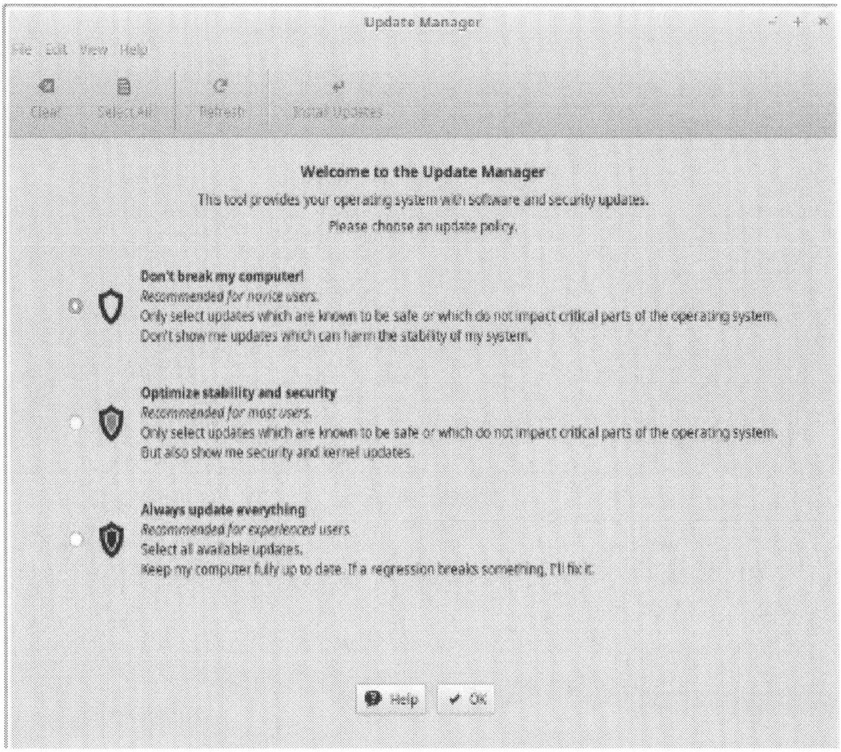
Update Manager
Welcome to the Update Manager
This tool provides your operating system with software and security updates.
Please choose an update policy.
Don't break my computer!
Recommended for novice users.
Only select updates which are known to be safe or which do not impact critical parts of the operating system.
Don't show me updates which can harm the stability of my system.
Optimize stability and security
Recommended for most users.
Only select updates which are known to be safe or which do not impact critical parts of the operating system.
But also show me security and kernel updates.
Always update everything
Recommended for experienced users.
Select all available updates.
Keep my computer fully up to date. If a regression breaks something, I'll fix it.
Help
OK

Once you have clicked on the icon for lock, the Update Manager will be opened and for the first time, you will be asked for the update policy which you need. You should then read through the available options and then choose the best one for you.

The majority of the users of Linux Mint like to have their software up to date, and they like to use the second option. However, for those who need the computer to work and then get all updates which are needed, you should choose the first option.

You will then be presented with the real update screen. You will also be asked whether you need to switch to some local mirror for the updates. Throughout the world, organizations exist which need to help Linux Mint in distributing updates to the world so that the users are able to get the best experience when using Linux Mint. For you to get the fastest updates, it will be good for you to choose the mirror which is near you. If you don't need to use a local mirror, then it is possible for you to change this below the Edit-Preferences.

The Update Manager will show you the updates which are available. The interface will be very easy for you to use. For each update done on the package, you will be in a position to read the description, change log which describes the changes which are made by the developers. If there are warnings from Linux Mint regarding the updates, you will also see the same. It is also possible for you to see the version which you have on your computer, as well as the one which you should update to. A symbol will also be shown, and this will specify whether it is a security or a package update.

The stability level which has been assigned to the package update will also be shown. Each update to the package usually brings some improvements or fixes to the security issues, but sometimes, bugs may occur. Linux Mint also assigns the stability level to each of the packages, and informs one of how safe they will be once they have applied the update.

It is possible for you to click on the columns and then sort them by status, stability level, version, or package name. The "Clear" and "Select All" buttons can be used for selecting or unselecting all the updates.

Both the Level 1 and the Level 2 updates are risk free, which means that you can go ahead and apply them. The Level 3 updates are expected to be "safe," and you should ensure that you have checked for them from the list of the updates. Whenever you experience any problem with a Level 3 update, it will be good for you to inform the Linux Mint development team so that the update can be made a Level 4 or Level 5 and others will be discouraged against applying it as a Level 3 update.

Choose Edit, Preferences, and then Level and you will see the screen given below:

Level	Description	Tested?	Origin	Safe?	Visible?
1	Certified updates. Tested through Romeo or directly maintained by Linux Mint.	✓	Linux Mint	☒	☒
2	Recommended updates. Tested and approved by Linux Mint.	✓	Upstream	☒	☒
3	Safe updates. Not tested but believed to be safe.	✗	Upstream	☒	☒
4	Unsafe updates. Could potentially affect the stability of the system.	✗	Upstream	☐	☐
5	Dangerous updates. Known to affect the stability of the systems depending on certain specs or hardware.	✗	Upstream	☐	☐

The default setting is that the Update Manager tells you more about the Level 1, , and 3 updates. One is free to make a decision on whether to make the Level 4 and Level 5 updates visible. If this is done, then more updates will appear on the list. It is also possible for you to make the Level 4 and the Level 5 updates to be "safe" if you want. However, this is not recommended, as doing that will cause the selection of these to be automatic on the Update Manager.

The Update Manager works by counting only the "safe" updates. If you are told that your system is up to date, it only means that there are no new updates which have been made for the level of update which you have assigned to be safe in your system. The Update Manager will only have the "visible" updates in its list.

A good example is when all of the levels have been made to be "visible," but only the Levels 1 and 2 have been marked to be "safe." In this case, a lot of updates will be seen in the list, and the Update Manager will be telling you that youf system is up to date.

The tab for "Options" gives you a number of choices by which you can alter the settings for the Update Manager.

You will also find the option "Include updates which requires the installation of new packages or the removal of installed packages" under Options and this will allow you to specify whether the Update Manager will be allowed to install some new dependencies or not. It is good for you to be careful whenever you are using this option as, although it may help you to install some new dependencies, it may also remove the ones which you have already installed.

The tab for "Auto-Refresh" will help you to define how often your Update Manager will be checking for updates. In the tab for "Ignored packages," you are able to define the packages for which you don't need to receive updates. The use of "*" and "?" is supported.

The tab for "Icons" allows you to change the icons used by the Update Manager in the system tray. In case the Update Manager gives you errors, you can proceed to check for the issue in the logs. Go to the system array, and right click on lock icon. Choose "Information," and you will see a new screen popup.

Chapter 5- Tips and Tricks

In Linux Mint, there are ways that one can perform the simplest tasks more easily. This will help you save on time. Let us discuss some of the tips and tricks in Linux Mint which can help you do this.

Copying and Pasting

In most cases, Linux Mint users have to select and then right click on the text which they need to copy. Others also do this by clicking on the "Edit" menu. This is time consuming. It is possible for you to copy and then paste the text that you want by use of the mouse only. In this case, the left button of the mouse will be responsible for copying the text, while the middle button will be responsible for pasting the text. That is very simple and time saving!

To demonstrate this, open a text editor or the LibreOffice Writer, or any application you like and which allows you to input some text. Type a few sentences into it. Use the left button of the mouse so as to select some of the text which you have just typed. Most do it by clicking on the "Edit" menu and then clicking on "Copy." Others also like to use some combination of keys such as "CTRL + COPY." Linux makes it simpler. By selecting a text, you will have copied it. Since you have already selected the text, it has been copied and kept in the "mouse buffer," and there is no need for you to press any other keys.

Click on some other part of the document so as to place your cursor there. Click on the middle button of the mouse. If your mouse has a wheel, just wheel-click while for those whose mouse has two buttons only, click the right and the left buttons together. You will observe that the text which you had just copied will be pasted.

If you get used to doing it, copying and pasting of text in Linux Mint will become easy for you. This also applies to the other Linux distributions.

It is good for you to note that the buffer which is used by the mouse is not the same as the one which is used by the Cinnamon desktop. This means that you can use your mouse to copy some text and then use the CTRL +C for copying another text or by the use of the "Edit" menu. This means that you will have copied two different items and the way you paste them will be determined by the way you copied them, either by use of the middle button of the mouse, the use of "CTRL + V," or by use of the "Edit" menu.

Taking Notes

Everyone likes taking notes when they are using the computer. One may also need to write something when they are using the computer, such as something they have been told via a phone. These are mostly the things which one needs to remember. Some people usually find themselves writing such notes on applications which are not suitable for such tasks. A good example is launching the LibreOffice writer so as to write a phone number. Linux Mint comes with a tool which is suitable for note-taking. This is known as "Tomboy Notes."

The tool is very easy to use as after you have just clicked on it, it will be launched with all your notes. If you need to take some new notes, you just have to click on "Create New Note." This will open up a new note.

Once you have changed the title for this, you will also have changed its name. You may choose to write whatever you need into the note and then close it. You will then be in a position to access the content which you have just written by use of Tomboy Notes. There will be no need or you to save the note, and you can even shut down and restart the computer without affecting the note. The note is saved immediately as you type it.

If you are done with the note and you are sure that you will not need to use it anymore, you can delete it by clicking on the "Delete" button. If you happen to write the title of a particular note in the note you are creating, then this second note will be opened once you have clicked on the link which will be created automatically by Tomboy. Tomboy Notes also allows you to use some formatting features as you create the note. Examples of these features include search features, synchronization, as well as exporting of notes to HTML, PDF, and others. That is how you can take notes in Linux Mint.

Conclusion

Linux Mint is one of the distributions of Linux. It is based on Ubuntu and Debian. With Linux Mint, one can do a lot. By now, you must be comfortable with the various aspects regarding the use of Linux Mint. The Linux Mint terminal can help you accomplish most of the tasks more easily and quickly. A good example is when you are performing an upgrade of your system. You can do this by use of just a simple command, as opposed to use of the GUI in which you will have to update each component of your system.

To the Linux Mint beginners, the use of the command line might seem to a bit complex, but it is good for you to begin practicing and you will get used to it with time. When it comes to updates in Linux Mint, they are classified in the range of Level 1 to Level 5. One has to specify the level at which the system will be "safe." If this is violated, then you will get a notification in terms of the updates which are currently available, and you will have the option of upgrading to that level.

Printed in Great Britain
by Amazon